Sheela-na-Gigs

Origins and Functions

Eamonn P Kelly

Country House, Dublin
in association with
The National Museum of Ireland

Published in 1996 by
Town House and Country House
Trinity House
Ranelagh
Dublin 6
Ireland

in association with The National Museum of Ireland

British Library Cataloguing in Publication Data. A catalogue record for this book is available from the British Library.

ISBN 0–946172–51–X

Acknowledgements
I wish to thank the following persons and institutions for making photographs available: Brendan Doyle, Valerie Dowling and Mary Cahill, National Museum of Ireland; Declan McGonagle and Ruth Ferguson, Irish Museum of Modern Art; Kenny Photo Graphics, Fethard, Co Tipperary; John Scarry, Heather King and Geraldine Stout, National Monuments Service; Albert Siggins, Roscommon County Museum; Leo Swan, Arch-Tech, Dublin. I wish to express my thanks to the following persons for assistance with research: Agnes O'Donovan, Research Assistant, and Erin Gibbons, Consultant Archaeologist. The distribution map was prepared by Michael Heffernan, National Museum of Ireland.

Typesetting: Red Barn Publishing, Skibbereen
Printed in Ireland by ßetaprint

CONTENTS

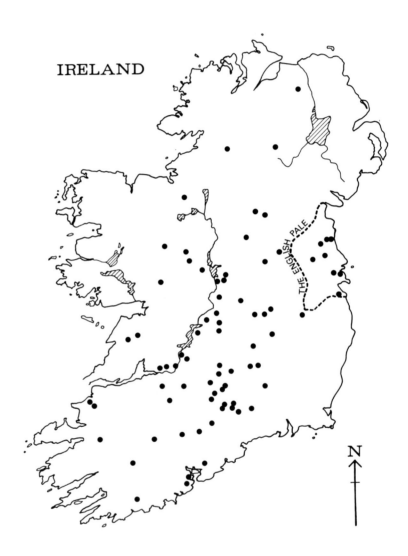

Figure 1. Map showing the distribution of sheela-na-gigs in Ireland.

IRELAND

N

INTRODUCTION

Sheela-na-gigs are carvings of naked females posed in a manner which displays and emphasises the genitalia. In recent decades interest in the figures has grown and they have often been a source of controversy. Sheela-na-gigs were first brought to scientific attention in the 1840s by antiquarians, some of whom regarded their aggressive sexuality in negative terms. More recently the images have come to be regarded in a positive light. By some they are seen as a symbol of Irishness and by others, particularly Irish feminists, they are a symbol of active female power.

The name 'sheela-na-gig' was first published in the Proceedings of the Royal Irish Academy 1840–44 as a local name for an exhibitionist carving which was once attached to the gable wall of a church at Rochestown, Co Tipperary. The name was recorded elsewhere in Tipperary in 1840 by John O'Donovan, an official of the Ordnance Survey, who referred to a figure on Kiltinane church, Co Tipperary (Photo 1&2), by this name. The stone in question was stolen in January 1990 (Photo 3). Recent research has shown that the name sheela-na-gig was in use as early as the seventeenth century, where it occurs in Catholic diocesan and provincial statutes. During the eighteenth century a Royal Navy vessel named HMS Shiela-na-gig was active in the West Indies.

The name sheela-na-gig comes from the Irish language, although its meaning is uncertain. The most likely interpretations are *Sighle na gCíoch*, meaning 'the old hag of the breasts', or *Síle-ina-Giob* meaning 'sheela (a name for an old woman) on her hunkers'. Other recorded names include the Devil Stone, the Idol, the Evil Eye Stone, Julia the Giddy, Shiela O'Dwyer, Cathleen Owen, St Shanahan, Whore, the Witch, and the Hag of the Castle.

No tradition or folklore has been recorded in Ireland which provides any useful insight into the origin or function of sheela-na-gigs, although

Photo 1. Medieval church, Kiltinane, Co Tipperary. From c. 1195 to the dissolution, the church belonged to St Mary's Abbey, Osney, Oxfordshire, England. A sheela-na-gig was placed horizontally on a quoin at the angle of the east gable.

Photo 2. Sheela-na-gig, medieval church, Kiltinane, Co Tipperary. This is the carving which John O'Donovan recorded in 1840 under the name 'sheela-na-gig'. The figure was stolen in 1990 and has not yet been recovered.

comparisons with similar figures which occur in Britain and on the Continent prove helpful in this respect.

HISTORICAL BACKGROUND

The second half of the eleventh century through to the end of the thirteenth century was a period of economic and social development throughout Europe, which led to increased urbanisation and population growth. It was also a time which saw the growth of papal power, together with the proliferation of new monastic orders under papal direction and protection. In England, the Norman invasion of 1066 resulted in an influx of continental religious orders which, within a century and a half, had built more than 1,000 religious houses. Between 1074 and 1111 — more than half a century before the invasion of Ireland — Anglo-Norman influence was an important factor in

Irish ecclesiastical affairs. This was particularly so in the Hiberno-Norse towns, whose bishops were often English trained.

Between 1070 and 1109, Lanfranc and his successor as Archbishop of Canterbury, Anselm, were deeply involved in matters affecting the Irish Church and consecrated a number of her bishops. They were concerned particularly with seeking reform of the ecclesiastical organisation of the Irish Church, but it is also clear that they disapproved strongly of certain aspects of Irish social life. In particular, the customary Irish law on divorce and remarriage — as well as the

Photo 3. Reward poster produced by the Fethard Historical Society.

Photo 4. Twelfth-century pilgrim's badge from Rome, found in Dublin. It bears the images of the Apostles Peter and Paul.

married status of Irish churchmen — was at odds with Roman practices and was regarded by Lanfranc and his Anglo-Norman contemporaries as a law of fornication, rather than a law of marriage. The Synod of Cashel in 1101 partially reformed Irish law by forbidding marriage among close kin, but, by failing to address the practices of concubinage and divorce, fell short of the requirements of Rome. That the Irish came to be regarded by outsiders as a sinful and licentious people reflected the fact that Irish society embodied a different world view to that which had developed within late Roman Europe and its feudal successor. Irish traditions received little understanding or sympathy from the papacy, which had set itself the task of achieving canonical uniformity throughout western Christianity.

Due to the efforts of reforming churchmen, such as St Malachy, a degree of reorganisation of the Irish Church took place during the first half of the twelfth century. There was also renewed contact with the papacy, and continental orders such as the Augustinians and Cistercians were introduced. That the papacy viewed such efforts as too little and too late is suggested by the permission to invade Ireland granted to Henry II by the English Pope Adrian IV — probably at the prompting of Canterbury. One objective of such an invasion would have been to bring the Irish Church into full accord with Roman practices.

Photo 5. Male exhibitionist figure on a corbel in Margam, Wales. Whereas male exhibitionist figures occur regularly on the Continent, in Ireland the emphasis is on female figures. The phallus is a symbol commonly employed on corbels in France. A rare example occurs on a carved window in Ballynagown Castle, a late medieval O'Brien tower house in Smithstown, Co Clare.

THE ROMANESQUE STYLE

In the period immediately prior to the Norman invasion of Ireland in 1169, renewed contact with Europe led to changes in religious architecture and sculpture in Ireland. It was a period when there was centralisation of political power in the hands of provincial dynasties who were patrons of the Church. This led to a renaissance in fine ecclesiastical metalwork, such as shrines and crosiers, as well as the construction of new churches.

In 1134, Cormac's Chapel was completed on the Rock of Cashel, thus heralding the introduction into Ireland of the Romanesque style (Pls 1–2). This was an architecture which prevailed throughout western

Europe, from the middle of the tenth century to the middle of the twelfth century, and its forms were largely determined by Roman prototypes. Characteristic of the style was the semicircular arch, frequently used in elaborate doorways, as well as wide pillars with decorated capitals (Pl 3). The style was widely employed for churches, cathedrals and monastic buildings by the various monastic orders which flourished at the time.

THE AGE OF PILGRIMAGE

This was a time of widespread pilgrimage to centres such as the important shrine of Santiago de Compostela in north-western Spain, and to Rome itself. Huge numbers of the faithful participated, and the works of medieval writers such as Chaucer suggest that the preoccupations of the pilgrims were sometimes more worldly than sublime.

Throughout the medieval Church, prominent among the deadly sins were avarice and lust. Whereas avarice was regarded mainly as a male sin, lust was a sin which pertained particularly to women. In Romanesque and, later, in Gothic art, lust was often portrayed as a naked woman whose breasts and genitalia were eaten by toads and serpents. This was an adaptation of an image, known in antiquity, of Tellus Mater, the Earth Mother, who was represented suckling snakes,

Photo 6. Thirteenth-century pilgrim's holy-water flask in the shape of a ship. The object was found in Dublin and came from the shrine of St Thomas à Becket at Canterbury.

ancient symbols of the earth. Classical representations provided inspiration for the development of Romanesque art. Goddesses whose depictions proved influential included Terra, Gaia, Cybele, Demeter and her daughter Persephone.

Throughout parts of medieval Europe, on the carved stonework of churches — particularly those situated along the pilgrimage routes — there developed a range of exhibitionist figures, both male and female, together with related carvings, whose function was to alert the faithful to the dangers of the sin of lust (Pls 6–7). The emphasis on the genitalia — which are usually enlarged — related to the Church's teaching that sinners were punished in hell through the bodily organs by which they had offended (Photo 5).

Particularly from the eleventh century onwards, many of the Irish also engaged in pilgrimages, not only to local shrines but to Rome, or to Santiago de Compostela to visit the shrine of St James. The pilgrims travelled on the ships returning to Bordeaux from Ireland as part of the wine trade and from there continued on foot along a well-used pilgrim route across the Pyrenees to Santiago de Compostela. Excavations at St Mary's Cathedral, Tuam, Co Galway, uncovered the graves of two people who had made the journey. The bodies were accompanied by scallop shells, which were the emblem of St James. Pilgrims also acquired special badges and holy water flasks as mementoes of their journeys (Photos 4 & 6), much in the way that modern visitors to the shrine at Knock, Co Mayo, might acquire a souvenir medal or a bottle of Knock water. Secular badges were also produced and, in

Photo 7. Acrobatic exhibitionist figure on the chancel arch of the Nun's Chapel, Clonmacnois. Figures of this type are common in Romanesque carvings on the Continent.

Photo 8. Carved Romanesque windowsill now inserted upside-down in the wall of Rath Blathmach church, Co Clare. The main decoration shows a panel of ornament with serpent heads and foliage. To one side there is an exhibitionist figure between affronted beasts. The carving may date to c. 1180.

parts of medieval Europe, particularly in the region of the low countries, these displayed a wide range of erotic subjects. The precise significance of these erotic representations remains controversial, but clearly they are further evidence of the medieval preoccupation with lust.

A number of pilgrimages by Irish kings, aristocrats, merchants and prominent churchmen have been recorded and it was on such a journey to Rome that St Malachy died at Clairvaux in 1148. Through such visits, the Irish became familiar with Romanesque architecture with its exhibitionist and related figures which, in due course, was introduced into Ireland.

Photo 9. Detail of exhibitionist figure, Rath Blathmach church, Co Clare.

EARLY EXHIBITIONIST FIGURES IN IRELAND

In Ireland, the earliest exhibitionist figures appear to be those associated with Romanesque buildings, one of the best known of which is that on the chancel arch of the Nun's Church, Clonmacnois (Pl 8), depicting a naked figure whose face is embraced by the legs (Photo 7). The figure is comparable with acrobatic figures found commonly in Romanesque contexts on the Continent. Other Irish Romanesque figures can be pointed to, such as that of a female, with widely splayed legs and sagging genitalia, on a door or window head from Toomregon, Co Cavan, and a portion of a comparable figure found at Aghalurcher, Co Fermanagh. At Rath Blathmach, Co Clare (Pl 9), there is a Romanesque lintel (Photo 8) which has an exhibitionist figure between affronted beasts (Photo 9).

Photo 10. The Rattoo exhibitionist figure is located beside an upper window. Illustrated is a replica in the National Museum of Ireland.

The only example of an exhibitionist figure to be found on a round tower (Pl 10) occurs beside an upper window at Rattoo, Co Kerry (Photo 10). The finely carved doorway (Pl 11) shows that the tower is of twelfth-century construction. At White Island, Co Fermanagh, an exhibitionist figure was inserted horizontally, with its head against the doorway of a late Romanesque church.

IRISH SHEELA-NA-GIGS

Photo 11. Sheela-na-gig built into the town wall, Thurles, Co Tipperary. The town was a medieval creation of the Butlers, Earls of Ormond.

The Normans introduced English Gothic art and architecture to Ireland, and the style spread during the thirteenth century, especially within the areas of Norman conquest. The fourteenth century was a period of war and calamity, resulting from the Bruce invasions of 1315–17 followed by the Black Death of 1348–50. During the century there was sustained Gaelic resurgence and a reversal in the fortunes of the Anglo-Irish colonists. When prosperity returned during the fifteenth century, there was a revival of building, but, in contrast with the thirteenth century, the architecture of the period did not draw upon the English Late Gothic style. Indeed, the area outside the Pale (Pl 12) appears to have had little direct contact with England. Instead, Irish masons produced their own style, which was an amalgam of past and present.

The most typical buildings of the fifteenth and sixteenth centuries were small castles, known as tower houses, which were the residences of the gentry, both Anglo-Irish and Gaelic alike. Unlike earlier Irish castles, tower houses were an internal development, the architectural characteristics of which were essentially Irish.

Photo 12. In 1992 a sheela-na-gig was discovered in the Church of Ireland graveyard at Rosenallis, Co Laois. A ruined church and the stump of a round tower are evidence of an early ecclesiastical site.

Skilled masons were active, such as those employed around 1500 in two workshops in the Kilkenny region who were engaged in carving fine funerary monuments. One of these workshops was led by an Irish sculptor named Rory O'Tunney — even though this was an area where there had been heavy Anglo-Norman settlement. The other workshop was known as the Ormond school, after the Earls of Ormond whose patronage it enjoyed. The Ormond school employed a deliberately retrospective Irish Late Gothic style which has been described as more neo-Romanesque than Gothic. The general area in which these two schools operated has a high concentration of sheela-na-gigs, although it is not certain that there is a direct connection between these two facts.

The vast majority of true sheela-na-gigs found in Ireland appear to date to the period after the Norman invasion and they occur, predominantly, in areas where there was heavy Anglo-Norman settlement (Fig 1). Whereas the earlier Romanesque figures may form part of a larger decorative scheme, post-invasion sheela-na-gigs are single figures which were set in isolation. About 100 such figures are known or recorded and, as was the case with the earlier Romanesque carvings, many were carved for the walls of medieval churches. They also occur on tower houses and two examples were placed on medieval town walls at Fethard (Pl 13) and Thurles (Photo 11), Co Tipperary. A small number of carvings are known from other locations, such as gates, wells and pillars, but many of these, together with examples on a bridge and a mill, are likely to be in secondary positions.

The collection of the National Museum of Ireland contains thirteen carvings, which were presented for safe keeping, having become detached for various reasons. The most recent acquisition was found in a graveyard in Rosenallis, Co Laois, in 1992 (Photo 12). A further dozen examples are in other museums or in private collections, and many more are

Photo 13. Sheela-na-gig found in the Figile river, Clonbulloge, Co Offaly. The legs are not represented. Large hands hold open the vulva and show the clitoris. Other pieces of medieval carved masonry were found in the river, suggesting the destruction of a medieval building somewhere in the immediate area.

unaccounted for, so that only a record of their former existence is known.

Many figures are badly defaced by the elements or by vandalism, so that it is now difficult to identify them positively. Destruction of the figures appears to have begun in the seventeenth century. Provincial statutes for Tuam dating to AD 1631 ordered parish priests to hide away sheela-na-gigs. Other carvings were also destroyed at this time, including a wooden effigy of St Mac Dara. That there may also have been wooden sheela-na-gigs in existence is suggested by diocesan regulations which were issued in Ossory and Waterford in AD 1676, ordering that sheela-na-gigs be burned. There are accounts of sheela-na-gigs being buried in relatively recent times and the discovery of a sheela-na-gig in the Figile river at Clonbulloge, Co Offaly (Photo 13), must surely represent a deliberate attempt to dispose of the figure.

Photo 14. Sheela-na-gig from a thirteenth-century parish church, Ballylarkin, Co Kilkenny. This is one of the most finely carved sheela-na-gigs in Ireland.

POSE

Photo 15. Sheela-na-gig, Clenagh Castle, Co Clare. The figure, which is rendered in simple outline, is placed on a quoin low down on the south-east angle of the tower.

The majority of sheela-na-gigs are carved on rectangular blocks of stone which are twice as high as they are broad. The general size range is between 40 cm and 60 cm in height. Perhaps the smallest example is one of two sheela-na-gigs from Scregg Castle, Co Roscommon, which is a mere 10 cm high. The figures may be carved in high or low relief, in false relief, or defined by incised lines. Many are carved roughly, but some examples, such as the Ballylarkin, Co Kilkenny, sheela-na-gig (Photo 14), are excellent examples of the stone-carver's craft.

Because many sheela-na-gigs are badly weathered, it may in some cases be difficult to state with certainty the precise pose. Some variation exists, but it is by no means certain whether there is any real significance to this. The figures appear to be evenly divided between those which seem to be standing, such as the Blackhall Castle, Co Kildare sheela-

na-gig (Photo 33), and those which may be seated, such as the Cashel, Co Tipperary, figure (Pl 4). The legs may be widely splayed, as at Clenagh Castle, Co Clare (Pl 14 & Photo 15), where the thighs and lower legs are at right angles. Alternatively, the thighs may be splayed but with the heels together, as in the figure from Carne Castle, Co Westmeath (Photo 16). In the case of figures from St Gobnat's Abbey, Ballyvourney, Co Cork; Newtown Lennan church, Co Tipperary (Photo 17); and Clonbulloge, Co Offaly (Photo 13), the legs appear not to have been represented at all.

The commonest position of the arms is with the hands placed in front, gesturing towards the abdomen or, more explicitly, towards the pudenda. In some cases, such as Leighmore church and Burgesbeg church, Co Tipperary (Photo 18), the hands are joined in front around the pudenda, while the figure from Cavan town (Photo 19) shows the hands gripping the pudenda. Both arms are placed behind the thighs at four castle sites: Ballyporty, Co Clare (Photo 20); Dunnaman, Co Limerick; Lixnaw, Co Kerry (Photo 21); and Ballynacarriga, Co Cork. On the sheela-na-gig believed to have come from a Dominican friary in

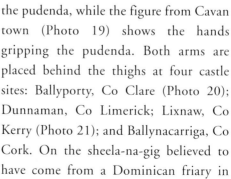

Photo 16. Sheela-na-gig found in the ruins of Carne Castle, Co Westmeath. This was a sixteenth-century tower house of the O'Melaghlin family, whose ancestors were kings of Meath.

Photo 17. Sheela-na-gig, Newtown Lennan, Co Tipperary. The figure was built into the wall of a church which contained elements dating back to the twelfth century.

Photo 18. Sheela-na-gig, now in the National Museum of Ireland, found in a graveyard at Burgesbeg, Co Tipperary. The parish is mentioned in tax returns of 1302, but the age of the church, of which little remains, is uncertain.

Clonmel, Co Tipperary (Photo 22), the right arm is behind the thigh while the left is in front, with both touching the pudenda.

A carving from a castle at Tinnakill, Co Laois, depicts the right hand raised to the head, with the left hand on the pudenda. The right hand rests on the right leg, with the left hand close to the pubic region, on a carving from Clonlara Castle, Co Clare. The pose is the same in the figure from Ballylarkin Church, Co Kilkenny (Photo 14), although, on this figure, one finger of the left hand rests on the pudenda in what may be a masturbatory gesture.

The arms embrace the thighs and knees in two Co Westmeath carvings: Taghmon church and the convent of St Peter's Port, Athlone, while at Tracton Abbey, Co Cork, the hands hang by the side. Both hands are raised on carvings at Castlemagner, Co Cork, and a fortified well at Kiltinane Castle, Co Tipperary (Photo 23–24). It has been suggested that the Taghmon, Tracton Abbey and

Photo 19. Sheela-na-gig, Cavan town. Said to be from an old church which no longer exists.

Castlemagner figures may not be regarded as true sheela-na-gigs. Certainly it is the case that, on most sheela-na-gigs, the hands are used to draw attention to the pudenda, in contrast with the carvings in question. However, the figure from Kiltinane Castle, Co Tipperary (Photo 24), is a true sheela-na-gig which appears to have an object in each raised hand. In the right hand there is a slender object, while the left hand holds a circular object, now damaged. Suggested identifications of the objects have included a dagger and a shield or, perhaps, a lucky horseshoe. On the Seir Kierán,

Photo 20. Sheela-na-gig found near Ballyporty Castle, Co Clare, a tower house dating to the late fifteenth or early sixteenth centuries.

cont. p 33

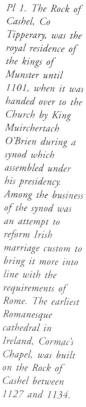

Pl 1. The Rock of Cashel, Co Tipperary, was the royal residence of the kings of Munster until 1101, when it was handed over to the Church by King Muirchertach O'Brien during a synod which assembled under his presidency. Among the business of the synod was an attempt to reform Irish marriage custom to bring it more into line with the requirements of Rome. The earliest Romanesque cathedral in Ireland, Cormac's Chapel, was built on the Rock of Cashel between 1127 and 1134.

Pl 2. Façade of Cormac's Chapel, Cashel, Co Tipperary.

Pl 3. Male face from a Romanesque capital, Cormac's Chapel, Cashel, Co Tipperary. The bulging eyes and gaping mouth are features which occur commonly on sheela-na-gigs.

*Pl 4. Sheela-na-
gig, Cashel, Co
Tipperary, which is
believed to have
the power to avert
the 'evil eye'.*

*Pl 4. Sheela-na-
gig, Cashel, Co
Tipperary, which is
believed to have
the power to avert
the 'evil eye'.*

*Pl 5. Male
exhibitionist figure
on a corbel in
Margam, Wales.*

Pl 6. Female
exhibitionist figure
in the Périgord
Museum, France.
The figure, which
is a caryatid, has
powerful features
similar to those
which occur on
Irish sheela-na-gigs.
The carving is
believed to have
come from the
church of St
Pierre-de-Pensac.

Pl 7. Exhibitionist
figure with both
male and female
attributes, Abbaye
de Daoulas,
Brittany, France.

Pl 8. Romanesque church known as the Nun's Chapel,
Clonmacnois, Co Offaly. The chapel was built by
Dervorgilla, wife of Tiernan O'Rourke. Her elopement
with Dermot Mac Murrough, King of Leinster, led to a
war and the banishment of Mac Murrough. The
Leinster king returned with Norman allies, and so
began the Norman invasion of Ireland. The Nun's
Chapel was completed in 1167, two years before the
invasion.

Pl 9. Medieval
nave-and-chancel
church of various
dates, Rath
Blathmach, Co
Clare.

Pl 10. The round tower at
Rattoo, Co Kerry, is the only
one in Ireland bearing an
exhibitionist figure.

Pl 11. The finely carved stonework of the doorway dates the Rattoo round tower to the twelfth century.

Pl 12. The Pale Ditch, Jamestown, Co Dublin, which enclosed a defended territory around Dublin known as 'the Pale' (from palisade). During the later Middle Ages, this was the main area of effective control by the English Crown in Ireland. The Irish and Anglo-Irish residing beyond the Pale developed a culture which drew upon elements from both traditions.

Pl 13. Sheela-na-gig inserted in the town wall, Fethard, Co Tipperary. The town came into being in the fourteenth century and permission was given in 1376 to enclose it with walls.

*Pl 14. Clenagh
Castle, Co Clare, a
late sixteenth-
century four-storey
tower house built
by the McMahons
of Clonderlaw.*

*Pl 15. Founded by
St Cíaráin, patron
saint of the
Kingdom of Ossory,
Seir Keirán, Co
Offaly, is an early
monastic enclosure
extending over 25
acres and
containing church
ruins, tombstones
and earthworks.
This former burial
place of the kings
of Ossory was
reorganised c.
1200 as a house of
the Canons
Regular of St
Augustine.*

Pl 16. Sheela-na-gig said to have been attached to a medieval church, Seir Kierán, Co Offaly. There are a series of holes drilled in the genital area and two further holes in the crown of the head. Their function is unknown and there is no evidence to support the view that they are connected with fertility cult practices.

*Pl 17–18.
Killinaboy church,
Co Clare. A
double-armed cross
of Lorraine built
into the gable
appears to date the
church to the
thirteenth century.
The remains of an
earlier round tower
are beside the
church.*

Pl 19a. A stone castle was built at Bunratty during the thirteenth century by the de Clare family, who were ousted by the native Irish during the fourteenth century. The present structure was erected about 1460. Until the early eighteenth century, Bunratty Castle was a dwelling place of the O'Briens, Earls of Thomond.

Pl 19b. Sheela-na-gig now placed in the window of the hall of the great keep, Bunratty Castle, Co Clare. Originally it was set in the inner reveal of a window in the south-west tower, which dates from the seventeenth century.

*Pl 20. Sheela-na-
gig in the wall of
Fethard Abbey, Co
Tipperary, an
Augustinian friary
founded shortly
after 1300.*

Pl 21. Sheela-na-gig, Rahara, Co Roscommon. The carving is on a keystone found in a graveyard beside a medieval church. Unlike most sheela-na-gigs, which are conspicuously bald, the Rahara figure is shown with two long plaited braids.

*Pl 22. Pillar on
which occurs a
weathered figure
believed to be a
sheela-na-gig, at
Tara, Co Meath.
The stone may
have flanked the
doorway of a
medieval church,
some of the
remains of which
are built into the
wall of the present
church.*

Pls 23–24. Sheela-na-gig on a quoin at the springing of the gable, north-east angle of the choir of Malahide Abbey. This is a fifteenth- to sixteenth-century manorial church of the Lords Talbot de Malahide. Dedicated to St Sylvester, it was the burial place of the Talbot family until the late nineteenth century. A second possible sheela-na-gig, now incomplete, is inserted in the east gable.

*Pl 25. Interest in
sheela-na-gigs has
grown in recent
years and they
have become a
subject for artists
and painters. The
figures have also
been used as a
subject for
jewellery, such as
this ceramic
brooch, based on
the sheela-na-gig
from Kiltinane
church, Co
Tipperary.*

cont. from p 16

Photo 21. Sheela-na-gig, Lixnaw, Co Kerry. Found in the bed of a river near The Court, a castle built in 1320 by Baron Lixnaw. His descendants, the Fitzmaurice family, occupied the castle into the eighteenth century.

Photo 22. Sheela-na-gig, Clonmel, Co Tipperary. Known as the 'Idol of Blue Anchor Lane', a reference to the place where it was discovered, in the wall of a bank in 1944. It is thought that the carving may, originally, have come from a Dominican priory in the grounds opposite.

Co Offaly, sheela-na-gig (Pls 15–16), a circular object is held by the right hand, in the genital area, while the sheela-na-gig from Lavey, Co Cavan (Photo 26), also shows a circular object which appears to be held between the left arm and the body. An interesting comparison with these figures is an exhibitionist figure on a quoin at Copgrove church, Yorkshire, which is depicted grasping a disc-shaped object in the right hand.

The circular object held by these figures is likely to be a mirror and the slender object held by the Kiltinane Castle figure (Photo 24)

Photo 23. Kiltinane Castle, Co Tipperary. The earliest reference to the castle dates to 1215. Beside the castle there is a fortified well which has a sheela-na-gig built into the wall.

Photo 24. Sheela-na-gig from a fortified well, Kiltinane Castle, Co Tipperary. Sheela-na-gigs usually show the hands pointing towards the pudenda. However, it may have been deemed appropriate to depict the figure with a mirror and comb when the sheela-na-gig was located near water, as such objects occur in Ireland on late medieval carvings of mermaids, which appear to be related to sheela-na-gigs.

may be a comb. Such objects are depicted on some Irish medieval mermaid figures which date to the fifteenth and sixteenth centuries. Nine are known and they occur in counties Kilkenny, Tipperary, Offaly, and Galway, which, as noted earlier, is the region where sheela-na-gigs are particularly common. Some are on churches which enjoyed the patronage of the Earls of Ormond (Photo 25). Representations of mermaids have a classical background and they occur frequently in European Romanesque contexts as symbols of vanity and lust. It is in this context that they also occur as a subject in Irish Late Gothic carvings, and their presence further underlines the neo-Romanesque character of the style.

Photo 25. Late fifteenth-century figure of a mermaid with a comb and mirror on a wall of Kilcooly Abbey, Co Tipperary. The wall also bears the arms of the Ormond Butlers.

OTHER FEATURES

It is clear that a deliberate effort has been made to represent sheela-na-gigs as grotesque, hideous and ugly. A particularly terrifying example is that from an old church near Cavan town (Photo 19) which is crisply carved and which exhibits a number of features. Like most of the sheela-na-gigs, it has a large head, and a series of emaciated ribs are clearly shown. Ribs are also present in examples from castles at Cullahill, Co Laois, at Scregg, Co Roscommon and Dunnaman, Co Limerick, and from churches at Killinaboy, Co Clare (Pls 17–18 & Photos 27–28), and Seir Kierán, Co Offaly (Pls 15–16). Breasts are rarely shown, but in those cases where they are present, such as on the Ballylarkin, Co Kilkenny, sheela-na-gig (Photo 14), they are small and usually accompanied by ribs, indicating emaciation.

Photo 26. Sheela-na-gig found in a graveyard in 1842 at Lavey, Co Cavan. It is believed to have come from the medieval parish church, which dates no earlier than the late twelfth century. Lavey church is dedicated to St Dymphna, an early Irish saint who is patroness of the insane.

Photos 27–28. Sheela-na-gig above the doorway of Killinaboy church, Co Clare.

Teeth are also shown on the Cavan sheela-na-gig (Photo 19) and they occur on a carving from a church at Lavey (Photo 26) in the same county. The Clonmel, Co Tipperary, sheela-na-gig (Photo 22) also appears to have teeth, as do examples found on castles at Bunratty, Co Clare (Pl 19 & Photo 29); Ballyporty, Co Clare (Photo 20); and Moate, Co Westmeath (Photo 31). The tongue protrudes in the cases of the sheela-na-gigs from Cavan town (Photo 19) and Cloghan Castle, Co Roscommon, while sheela-na-gigs from Ballynahinch Castle, Co Tipperary; Taghmon, Co Westmeath; and Clonbulloge, Co Offaly (Photo 13), have gaping mouths.

Most sheela-na-gigs have bulging or bossed eyes, an exception being the Ballylarkin, Co Kilkenny, carving (Photo 14), which is almost oriental in its facial expression. This figure also has prominent semicircular ears, at right angles to the head, which is a feature also present on the Ballyporty Castle, Co Clare (Photo 20); Fethard Abbey, Co Tipperary (Pl 20); Scregg Castle, Co Roscommon; and Kilsarkan, Co Kerry, sheela-na-gigs. Similar ears are shown on the Cullahill Castle, Co Laois, sheela-na-gig, but, as this carving is in high relief, the ears are depicted flat against the head. Originally, the Cavan town sheela-na-gig (Photo 19) had two ears, one of which has been broken off. These were more pointed than the earlier examples, and they are comparable to ears carved on the Seir Kierán, Co Offaly, sheela-na-gig (Pl 16).

A small number of sheela-na-gigs show striations on the cheeks or brows, which may represent wrinkles or perhaps tattoos. Examples include carvings from Cavan town (Photo 19), Clonbulloge (Photo 13) and Seir Kierán (Pl 16), both in Co Offaly, and two Co Tipperary examples, one located on the town wall in Fethard (Pl 13) and a second in Fethard Abbey (Pl 20).

Most sheela-na-gigs are conspicuously bald, although hair is represented on some. The keystone from Rahara church,

Co Roscommon (Pl 21), shows a sheela-na-gig with two long, braided plaits extending to the elbows and a similar figure is known from Castle Widenham, Co Cork. These two figures relate to the sheela-na-gig from Ballinderry Castle, Co Galway, which shows braided plaits attached to the head at right angles. It has been suggested that antlers or a head-dress are present on the badly eroded figure from Tara, Co Meath (Pl 22 & Photo 32); however, this may also be a representation of hair roughly in the manner of the figures already discussed. The mermaid figures mentioned earlier are usually depicted with long tresses on either side of the head, and influence from them may account for the hairstyle on these sheela-na-gigs. Another example where hair is depicted is that at Kilsarkan, Co Kerry, where the hair is represented by a cable-moulding across the top of the head. In the examples from Moate, Co Westmeath (Photos 31–31), and Cavan town (Photo 19), the hairstyle is represented in less specific terms.

The sheela-na-gig from Seir Kierán, Co Offaly (Pl 16), has two holes drilled into the crown of the head and it has been suggested that these were designed to hold a head-dress of some sort. Further holes of different sizes are drilled into the abdominal area. The figure is enigmatic and it has been suggested that the various holes may have performed some function in a fertility rite associated with the stone. There is no concrete evidence to support this speculation, however, and it is perhaps significant that the figure in question is detached. The possibility exists, therefore, that the holes were drilled some time after the stone became dislodged, though the reason for producing them remains a mystery.

Evidence exists to support the view that some sheela-na-gigs may have come to be regarded as having beneficial powers to assist fertility, but these beliefs appear to be of relatively recent folk origin. The carved

*Photo 33. Sheela-
na-gig, Blackhall
Castle, Co Kildare.
The castle dates to
the thirteenth
century, with later
additions and
alterations. The
sheela-na-gig is
placed by a
doorway set in
bricks of recent
date.*

Photo 34. Sheela-na-gig on a pillar which was used as a gate-post at Drynam, near Swords Glebe, Co Dublin. There are a number of ruined medieval buildings in the general vicinity and the stone may originally have flanked the doorway of one of them.

figure beside a holy well at Castlemagner, Co Cork, bears scratched pebble marks, cross shaped, on both hands, on the forehead, on the stomach above the navel and on the thighs. Over a window of Kilsarkan church, Co Kerry, there is a carving which shows evidence of rubbing of the genital area, but the practice is reported to be of recent vintage. A female figure over a window at St Gobnet's Abbey, Co Cork, has been treated similarly by visitors, although the practice appears to be longer established than is the case with the Kilsarkan figure. St Gobnet is an important Early Christian female saint associated with sites throughout Munster and the Aran Islands. Her foundation at Ballyvourney was a centre for pilgrimage throughout the medieval period and devotion to her remains strong today. The main attributes associated with the saint are the restoration of health and protection against illness.

THE LOCATIONS OF THE FIGURES

The majority of known or recorded sheela-na-gigs are no longer in primary positions on the buildings for which they were originally carved. Nevertheless, it can be observed that examples were commonly placed on the quoins of castles, as demonstrated by examples at Ballyfinboy, Co Tipperary, and Clenagh, Co Clare (Pl 14 & Photo 15). These were inserted vertically into the walls, but a number of quoins from castle sites, although carved to represent standing or squatting figures, have been inserted in a horizontal or reclining position reminiscent of the White Island, Co Fermanagh, exhibitionist figure referred to earlier.

Other examples of reclining figures include sheela-na-gigs from Cloghan, Co Roscommon; Doon Castle, Co Offaly; Tullavin Castle, Co Limerick; and Clomantagh Castle, Co Kilkenny. It might be

Photo 35. Detail of the Drynam sheela-na-gig.

Photo 36. Sheela-na-gig found near Birr, Co Offaly. The figure is unusual in Ireland, in that it was carved on a corbel. In England and on the Continent, exhibitionist figures were a common feature on corbels.

suggested that this practice indicates a re-use of sheela-na-gigs, and that the figures may have been removed from churches for re-use in secular buildings. This appears not to have been the case, however, as the pattern appears to be the same on churches. A sheela-na-gig on a quoin at Kiltinane church, Co Tipperary (Photos 1–2), was inserted horizontally, while that from Malahide Abbey, Co Dublin (Pls 23–24), was in a vertical position. A stone, now in the National Museum of Ireland, from Lavey church, Co Cavan (Photo 26), may also be a quoin, but the manner of its former attachment is uncertain.

Examples of the positioning of sheela-na-gigs over or beside the doorways of buildings can be demonstrated. The keystone of the doorway of Ballinderry Castle, Co Galway, bears a sheela-na-gig and another occurs on a keystone from Scregg Castle, Co Roscommon, now built into a nearby carriage-house. The stone referred to earlier from Rahara church, Co Roscommon (Pl 21), was dislodged when found, but its identification as a keystone appears secure. Sheela-na-gigs were also placed above or beside the doorways of castles at Timahoe, Co Laois; Ballynahinch, Co Tipperary; and Blackhall Castle, Co Kildare (Photo 33). A sheela-na-gig was placed above the gateway of the convent of St Peter's Port, Athlone, Co Westmeath, and another is located over the door of a church at Killinaboy, Co Clare (Pls 17–18 & Photo 27). A further example is found inside the door of Leighmore church, Co Tipperary.

A pillar-stone which stands beside the church at Tara, Co Meath (Pl 22 & Photo 32), bears a badly weathered figure, believed to be a sheela-na-gig. The stone may have flanked the doorway of a ruined medieval church, some of the carved stonework of which can be seen built into the wall of the modern church. A pillar-stone from Drynam, Swords Glebe, Co Dublin (Photos 34–35), now in the National Museum of Ireland, may have had a similar function. At Bunratty Castle (Pl 19 & Photo 29), a sheela-na-gig was placed in the inner reveal of a window, while at St Gobnat's Abbey, Ballyvourney, Co Cork, and Kilsarkan church, Co Kerry, sheela-na-gigs were placed over windows. At Moygara Castle, Co Sligo, a figure identified as a sheela-na-gig was carved on a corbel-stone which was once on a barbican. A sheela-na-gig also occurs on a corbel-stone from Birr, Co Offaly (Photo 36), but the building it once formed part of is not known.

In some cases, such as at Ballynacarriga Castle, Co Cork, Dunnaman Castle, Co Limerick, and Cullahill Castle, Co Laois, the figures are simply placed high up on the external tower walls. On churches at Rochestown, Co Tipperary, and Seir Kierán, Co Offaly (Pls 15–16), figures were placed on gable walls, while other walls were chosen to display sheela-na-gigs at Dowth Old Church, Co Meath, and in two Co Tipperary abbeys: Fethard (Pl 20) and Holycross. At Abbeylara, Co Longford, a badly weathered figure, possibly a sheela-na-gig, was placed in an unusual position, on an inside wall of a Cistercian tower.

Some sheela-na-gigs do not form part of the architecture of church buildings but, nevertheless, have religious associations. Included here are an example in Kildare Cathedral carved on the tomb of Bishop Wellesley which dates to AD 1539 and a sheela-na-gig carved on a free-standing stone cross at Stepaside, Co Dublin. A sheela-na-gig placed at St Flannan's Well, Killaloe, Co Clare, and the doubtful carving beside a holy well at Castlemagner, Co Cork, appear not to be in primary positions, although the figure built into a fortified well at Kiltinane Castle, Co Tipperary (Photo 24), may be in an original setting.

CONCLUSIONS

An assessment of the buildings on which they occur suggests that Irish sheela-na-gigs date to the period between the thirteenth and seventeenth centuries. The sheela-na-gig from the Convent of St Peter's Port, Athlone, Co Westmeath, may date to around AD 1200, while the Killinaboy, Co Clare, sheela-na-gig (Photos 27–28) is placed over the doorway of what appears to be a thirteenth-century church (Pls 17–18). It may be significant that, where the original provenances of the small group of sheela-na-gigs found within the Pale are known, all appear to have religious associations.

Sheela-na-gigs found on castles have a similar but slightly more restricted distribution to those found on churches and the earliest of them appear to be generally later in date than examples found on churches. A carving of a sheela-na-gig from Ballinderry Castle, Co Galway, erected shortly after AD 1540, is decorated with marigold and triskele motifs which are characteristic of the Celtic revival art of the period. The Moate, Co Westmeath, figure (Photos 30–31) was inserted in a wall over an entrance believed to have been built as late as AD 1649. These factors may indicate that there was a change, over time, in the perceived meaning and function of sheela-na-gigs. Their primary function on churches appears to have been as invocations against lust. Subsequently, during the later Middle Ages when the figures began to be placed on secular buildings, they came to be regarded as protective icons. The main reason for this development may be found in the cultural assimilation of the Anglo-Normans in all areas outside the Pale during a time of Gaelic resurgence, from the late thirteenth to the sixteenth century.

In a European feudal context, the function of sheela-na-gigs was one which portrayed a negative view of women's sexuality, but the evidence suggests that this view was not fully endorsed by the native Irish or, later, by the gaelicised Anglo-Irish. In pagan times the principal goddess was Anu, an earth goddess attested in many parts of Europe who is of primitive Celtic or even Indo-European derivation. Local variations of her cult gave rise to a variety of other names which could equally be applied to a patroness of agriculture and productivity.

During the Middle Ages, the adoption of Irish ways, laws, language and literature made a deep impact upon the world view of the Anglo-Irish colonists, of whom it was said that they became 'more Irish than the Irish'. The truth of this statement may be judged by the fact that FitzGerald, Earl of Desmond (1363–98), is regarded as the first great love poet in the Gaelic language, an achievement which would have required great familiarity with the Irish language and culture.

The Irish literary and intellectual tradition, which was adopted by the Anglo-Irish, developed without interruption into the seventeenth century. The ancient tales, such as the epic 'Táin Bó Cúalnge' or 'Cattle Raid of Cooley', versions of which are to be found in a number of manuscripts dating to the Middle Ages, were an important component of this learned tradition. The epic contains a number of female characters, such as Medb, Queen of Connacht, the prophetess Fedelm, and Morrigan — a war goddess — the actions of whom are central to the development of the tale. To these figures can be added others, such as Brighid, Macha, Áine, Aoibhieall and Clíona, all of whom are a metaphor for the land.

Throughout the medieval period, the poets used the conceit that their patron lords were spouses of their territories and the theme was maintained as a poetic convention into the nineteenth century with Ireland — called Éire, Banba or Fodla — appearing to poets in visions complaining that she had been deprived of her spouse and defiled by foreign usurpers. It is within this context that a reinterpretation of exhibitionist figures in later medieval Ireland took place.

The possible psychological impact of the calamities of the fourteenth century should not be overlooked. In their original meaning the sheela-na-gigs were protective icons, in that they were employed to protect men from eternal damnation by issuing a timely warning against the sin of lust. The manner in which this function was expanded to serve as a general protection against evil can be understood easily in the particular circumstances which prevailed in Ireland during the later Middle Ages.

Sheela-na-gigs are powerful images and popular interest in them has grown since their rediscovery by antiquarians during the last century (Pl 25). Contemporary interest tends to lay stress on the positive aspects of female sexuality and, in particular, on the reproductive function. Such an interpretation is perhaps closer to the function of the classical models out of which sheela-na-gigs arose than was the case with the exhibitionist figures carved in European male-dominated feudal society. In the context of Ireland, this process of redefinition has been on-going since the figures were first introduced during the twelfth century.

RECOMMENDED READING

Andersen, J. 1977. *The Witch on the Wall*. Rosenkilde and Bagger. Copenhagen.

Cherry, S. 1992. *A Guide to Sheela-na-Gigs*. National Museum of Ireland, Dublin.

Guest, E M. 'Irish Sheela-na-Gigs' in *Journal of the Royal Society of Antiquaries of Ireland*, 66, 107–29.

Weir, A and Jerman, J. 1986. *Images of Lust: Sexual Carvings on Medieval Churches*. Batsford. London.